8

I can cut and stick

Ray Gibson

Designed by Amanda Barlow
Illustrated by Michaela Kennard
Edited by Jenny Tyler
Photography by Howard Allman

and Ray Moller

Contents

Make a truck

Stick on a window

1. Cut some squares as big as this book.

2. Fold one in half and in half again. Cut along the folds.

3. Stick down two big squares and one small one.

Decorate with
strips of paper.
Stick on letters
from magazines.

4. Cut some wheels
from dark paper.

5. Stick them on.
Add foil hub caps.

Make a caterpillar

1. Open out the flap of an envelope.

2. Fold in half. Cut a "V" to fit your finger.

3. Cut off the corners.

4. Open out. Sponge paint on both sides.

4

Stick
fingers
through
holes.

5. Cut eyes and
a big smile from
paper. Stick
them on.

Make flowers and bees

1. Draw a flower with a wax crayon.

2. Cut it out. Stick on a paper middle.

3. Make some more flowers and leaves.

6

4. Draw bees. Crayon eyes and stripes. Cut bees out.

Stick the wings on the bees.

5. Draw wings. Cut them out.

6. Stick everything down in a pattern.

Make a snake card

1. Fold a long piece of cardboard in half.

2. Cut a long strip of gift wrap. Fold in half.

3. Fold in half again. Then open out.

4. Cut the corners off at one end. Cut a point at the other.

5. Turn over. Put glue on both ends.

6. Stick inside the card. Let it dry. Add paper eyes.

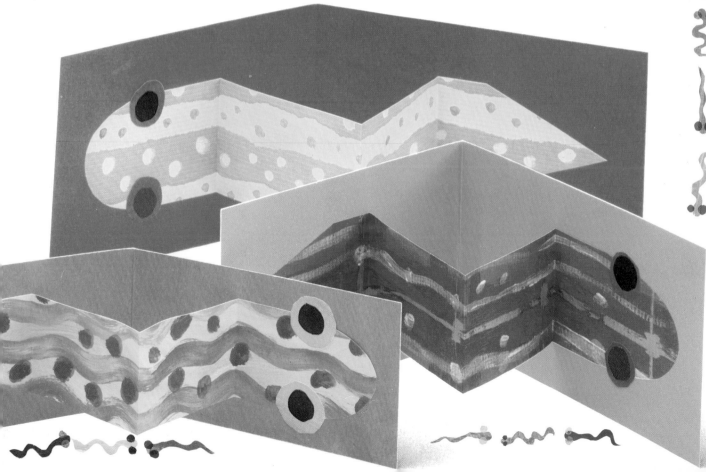

Make a crown

1. Fold a gold or silver doily in half.

2. Cut a strip of folded foil to fit around your head.

3. Put the folded foil inside the doily.

4. Open the doily. Put glue all around the bottom edge.

5. Fold it again, with the foil inside, so the sides stick.

6. Stick on scraps of shiny paper, ribbon, and crumpled tissue.

Tape the
crown to fit
your head

If you don't
have a gold or
silver doily, dab
paint on a
white one.

Make a hanging fish

1. Draw a fish shape on bright paper.

2. Cut it out. Glue on an eye.

3. Cut some strips. Glue them on.

Tape on a
string to
hang your
fish up.

4. Stick on some
shapes. Cut off what
you don't need.

5. Cut some paper
spikes. Glue them at
the top.

6. Cut long pieces of
tissue paper for a
tail. Stick them on.

Make a bonfire

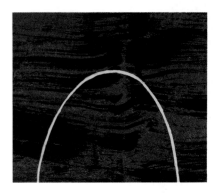

1. Cut red, orange and yellow shapes from magazines or giftwrap.

2. Cut into flame shapes. Make the ends pointed.

3. Draw a tall shape like a hill on dark paper.

4. Stick yellow flames at the top, orange flames below, then red.

5. Fill the spaces with leftover flames. Add black sticks. Cross them over.

6. Use wisps of cotton ball for smoke, and kitchen foil pieces and stars for sparks.

Make a spoon princess

1. Paint the back of a wooden spoon.

2. Cut cloth as wide as this book and as tall as your spoon.

3. Wrap it around the spoon. Tape at the top.

4. Fasten it on with a rubber band.

You could
stick on
sequins.

5. Tape knitting yarn
to the back, then
sides of the head.

6. Cut out and stick
on a paper crown.
Draw on a face.

Make an octopus puppet

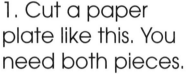

1. Cut a paper plate like this. You need both pieces.

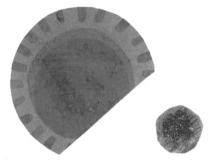

2. Turn the big piece over. Use a sponge to wipe green paint all over.

3. Wipe green paint on both sides of a sheet of strong paper. Roll it up.

4. Cut the roll into pieces, like this. Then unroll them.

5. Stick them to the unpainted side of the plate.

6. Tape the small piece of plate to the back, for a handle.

Stick on paper
eyes and a
mouth.

You can add
some patterns
to your
octopus.

Make a big bug

Paint these too.

1. Cut a cardboard egg carton in two. Paint both pieces.

2. Cut the round parts from another carton, for feet.

3. Cut three pipe-cleaners in half. Stick them to the feet.

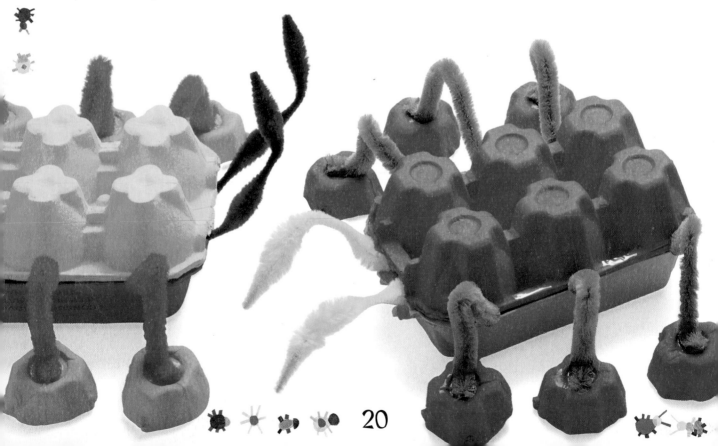

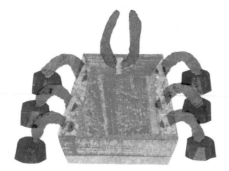

4. Tape these inside the flat part of the egg carton.

5. Fold a pipe-cleaner and stick it on for feelers.

6. Stick the bumpy egg carton lid on top to finish off.

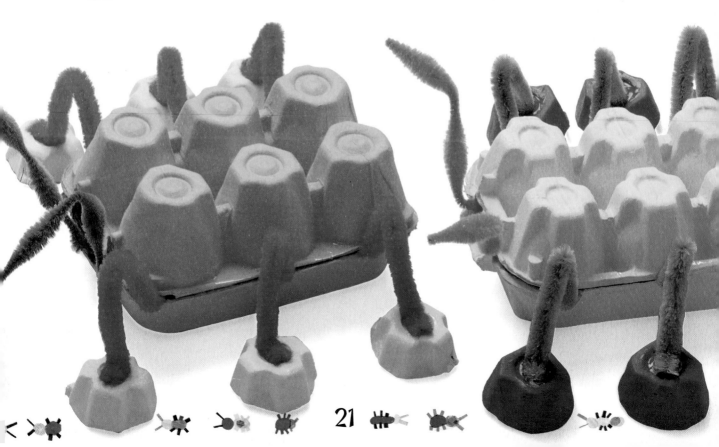

Make a snow picture

1. Cut a cardboard circle. Paint it blue.

2. Cut tree parts from brown paper. Stick them on.

3. Cut green cloth or paper. Stick on for bushes.

4. Stick on pieces of cotton ball for snow and a snowman.

5. Add a hat, scarf and face cut from paper or cloth.

6. Stick on a kitchen foil moon, and some icicles on the tree.

Tape on a loop
for hanging.

Make a pecking bird

1. Fold a paper plate. Unfold. Paint stripes on the back.

2. Fold it again. Stick a paper beak inside.

3. Cut some paper into spikes.

4. Stick them on the head. Add an eye.

Cut feather shapes and stick them on if you like.

5. Cut strips of bright tissue as long as your hand.

6. Twist them together. Tape them at the back for a tail.

Rock your bird to make it peck.

Make a necklace

1. Cut some paper as long as a straw. Glue the back.

2. Lay the straw in the middle. Press hard.

3. Fold the paper over the straw so the edges meet.

You could use giftwrap.

4. Press the paper hard. Let it dry. Cut it into pieces.

5. Cut shapes in the paper. Make some more.

6. Thread onto thick yarn with a big needle.

Tie the ends to fit around your neck or wrist.

Make a firework

1. Stick bands of paper around a toilet roll.

2. Add some sticky shapes.

3. Stick red and yellow paper onto kitchen foil. Let it dry.

4. Cut this paper into thin pieces.

5. Stick the strips inside the top.

Use a kitchen paper towel roll for a big firework.

29

Make a big-nosed clown

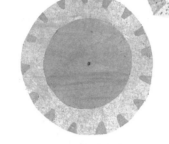  

1. Poke a hole in a paper plate with a pencil.

2. Wipe the back all over with bright paint. Let it dry.

3. Stick on two buttons for eyes, and a paper mouth.

4. Cut up some bright yarn and glue it on for hair.

5. Cut shapes for a hat from cardboard or a box.

6. Stick on a flower from a magazine or seed packet.

7. Get help to blow up a balloon a little way.

8. Poke it through the hole. Tape it at the back.

His nose will
wobble if you
shake his head.

31

Make a brooch

1. Draw a pig like this on stiff paper.

2. Cut it out. Stick on a button nose.

3. Tape a safety pin on the back.

You could make a fish...

...or a cat...

...or a flower.

First published in 1996 by Usborne Publishing Ltd, 83-85 Saffron Hill, London EC1N 8RT, England.
Copyright © Usborne Publishing Ltd. The name Usborne and the device ⛲ are Trade Marks of Usborne Publishing Ltd.

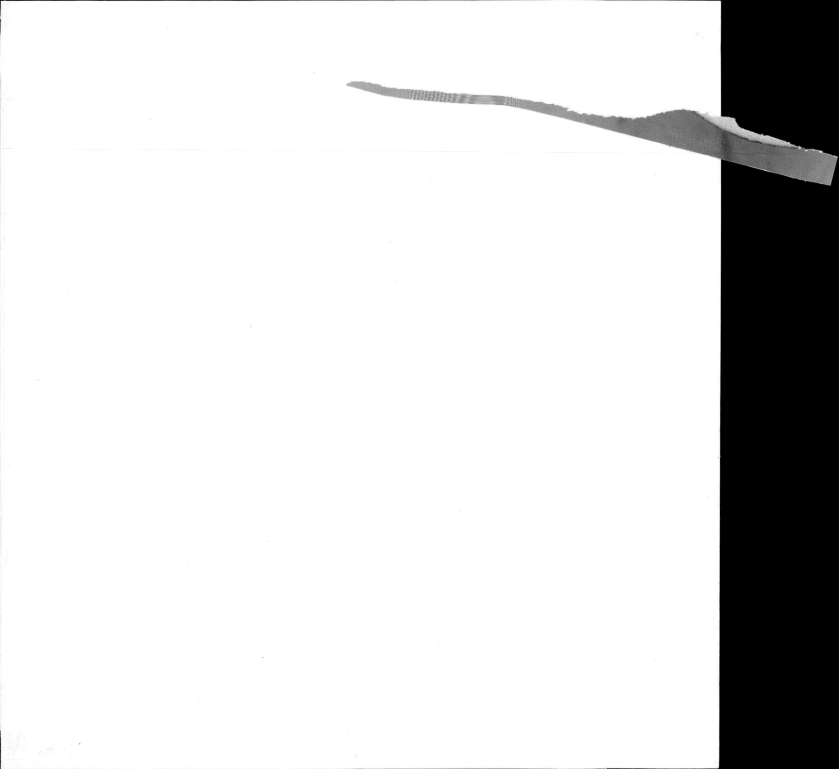